DIGITAL MARKETING SIMPLIFIED

"Mastering the Art of Online
Success in a Digital World"

VINCENT SIMS

Moral Rights

Vincent Sims asserts the moral right to be identified as the author of this work.

External Content

Vincent Sims has no responsibility for the persistence or accuracy of URLs for external or third-party Internet Websites referred to in this publication and does not guarantee that any content on such Websites is, or will remain, accurate or appropriate.

Dedication

"To all aspiring digital marketers, may this book illuminate your path and simplify the complexities of the digital landscape. Your passion for mastering the art of online influence inspires this guide. Here's to transforming challenges into opportunities and making your mark in the dynamic realm of digital marketing."

Table of Contents

Acknowledgments

"I extend my heartfelt gratitude to the tireless individuals who contributed to the creation of this book, 'Digital Marketing Simplified.' Special thanks to my mentors and industry experts whose insights shaped these pages. My appreciation also goes to the dedicated team who supported this endeavor, and to every reader – your curiosity fuels the ever-evolving world of digital marketing. Together, we simplify and innovate."

Preface

Welcome to "Digital Marketing Simplified." In the vast and ever-changing landscape of online promotion, this book is crafted as a compass to navigate the complexities with ease. Whether you're a seasoned marketer seeking clarity or a novice eager to dive in, these pages are designed to demystify the digital realm.

As we embark on this journey, envision a guide that transcends jargon, breaks down barriers, and empowers you to harness the full potential of digital marketing. Drawing from practical experiences, industry trends, and innovative strategies, this book aims to equip you with the knowledge and confidence to thrive in the dynamic digital ecosystem.

In each chapter, we unravel key concepts, share actionable insights, and provide real-world examples that bridge theory and practice. Consider this your handbook for mastering the art of online influence.

Thank you for choosing to explore the world of digital marketing with us. May your journey be both enlightening and rewarding.

Happy reading,
[Vincent Sims]

Foreword

In an era where digital landscapes evolve at breakneck speed, "Digital Marketing Simplified" emerges as a beacon of clarity in a sea of complexity. As I delve into the pages of this enlightening guide, it becomes evident that the author's commitment to simplification is not just a promise but a guiding philosophy.

In the world of digital marketing, where trends can be as elusive as they are transformative, this book stands out as a roadmap, guiding both novices and experts alike through the intricacies of online influence. It seamlessly blends theoretical foundations with hands-on strategies, providing a comprehensive resource for anyone seeking to navigate and thrive in the digital sphere.

The author's expertise, evident throughout, is matched only by their passion for demystifying the often daunting concepts that accompany digital marketing. Each chapter is a journey, each page a revelation, and by the end, readers will find themselves not only informed but equipped to face the challenges and embrace the opportunities of our digital age.

As we embark on this expedition through the digital realm, let "Digital Marketing Simplified" be your trusted companion. It is more than a guide; it's a testament to the transformative power of knowledge in our ever-evolving digital landscape.

Here's to clarity, innovation, and the boundless possibilities of digital marketing.

[Vincent Gill]
[Relationship Psychologist]

Chapter 1

Introduction to Digital Marketing

- Understanding the Basics

Digital marketing is a dynamic and integral component of modern business strategies. At its core, it involves leveraging digital channels, platforms, and technologies to promote products or services. Understanding the basics of digital marketing is crucial for businesses aiming to thrive in the online landscape.

Key elements of digital marketing include search engine optimization (SEO), where the goal is to enhance a website's visibility on search engines; social media marketing (SMM), which involves promoting products or services on platforms like Facebook, Instagram, and Twitter; and email marketing, a targeted approach to reaching and engaging potential customers.

Additionally, pay-per-click (PPC) advertising allows businesses to place ads on search engines and pay a fee each time their ad is clicked. Content marketing focuses on creating and distributing valuable content to attract and retain a target audience. Analytics plays a vital role, as digital marketers use data to measure the effectiveness of their campaigns and make informed decisions for optimization.

In essence, digital marketing provides a comprehensive toolkit for businesses to connect with their audience in the online realm, driving brand awareness, customer engagement, and ultimately, business growth.

- Evolution of Digital Marketing

The evolution of digital marketing traces a fascinating journey, mirroring the rapid advancements in technology and shifts in consumer behavior over the years.

1. Early Internet Era:

In the 1990s, as the Internet became accessible to the masses, the initial form of digital marketing emerged. Basic websites and email campaigns marked the early attempts to connect with online audiences.

2. Search Engine Dominance:

The early 2000s saw the rise of search engines like Google. This era emphasized the importance of search engine optimization (SEO) and pay-per-click (PPC) advertising, paving the way for businesses to optimize their online presence.

3. Social Media Explosion:

With the advent of social media platforms like Facebook, Twitter, and Instagram in the mid-2000s, digital marketing shifted towards social media marketing. Brands started engaging with audiences on a more personal level, creating a two-way communication channel.

4. Mobile Revolution:

The increasing use of smartphones transformed digital marketing yet again. Mobile apps and responsive web design became crucial, and location-based marketing gained prominence, targeting users based on their geographical location.

5. Content is King:

In the latter part of the 2000s and into the 2010s, content marketing took center stage. Valuable and relevant content became a key strategy to attract and retain customers. Blogging, video marketing, and other content formats gained traction.

6. Data-Driven Marketing:

As big data and analytics capabilities expanded, marketers began relying on data-driven insights to refine and optimize their strategies. This era emphasized the importance of measuring campaign performance and making data-backed decisions.

7. Artificial Intelligence (AI) Integration:

The current landscape witnesses the integration of artificial intelligence into digital marketing. AI algorithms analyze vast amounts of data, enabling marketers to personalize content, predict consumer behavior, and enhance the overall customer experience.

8. Video Dominance and Influencer Marketing:

Video content has become a dominant force, with platforms like YouTube and TikTok gaining immense popularity. Influencer marketing has also emerged as a powerful strategy, leveraging the reach and credibility of online influencers.

9. Ephemeral Content and Interactive Experiences:

Platforms like Snapchat and Instagram Stories introduced the concept of ephemeral content, emphasizing real-time and temporary engagement. Interactive experiences, such as polls and quizzes, have become essential for audience engagement.

10. Privacy Concerns and Regulation:

Recent years have seen an increased focus on user privacy and data protection. Regulations like GDPR and increased scrutiny of data practices have prompted marketers to prioritize ethical and transparent approaches.

The evolution of digital marketing continues to unfold, shaped by technological innovations, changing consumer expectations, and the ever-shifting digital landscape. Staying abreast of these developments is vital for marketers aiming to navigate the dynamic world of digital promotion successfully.

- Key Concepts and Terminology

Understanding key concepts and terminology is essential for anyone venturing into the realm of digital marketing. Here's a concise overview of some fundamental terms:

1. SEO (Search Engine Optimization):
   The process of optimizing online content to improve its visibility on search engine results pages (SERPs). This involves using relevant keywords,

creating high-quality content, and enhancing website structure.

2. SEM (Search Engine Marketing):

A broader term that encompasses SEO but also includes paid search advertising. SEM strategies aim to increase a website's visibility through both organic and paid means.

3. PPC (Pay-Per-Click):

An advertising model where advertisers pay a fee each time their ad is clicked. Commonly associated with search engine advertising, platforms like Google Ads use PPC as a pricing model.

4. Social Media Marketing (SMM):

The use of social media platforms to connect with an audience, build brand awareness, and drive website traffic. SMM involves creating and sharing content on platforms like Facebook, Instagram, Twitter, and LinkedIn.

5. Content Marketing:

The creation and distribution of valuable, relevant content to attract and engage a target audience. Content marketing aims to build brand authority and foster long-term relationships with customers.

6. Email Marketing:

The use of email to communicate with a target audience. Email marketing campaigns can include newsletters, promotional offers, and personalized content to nurture leads and retain customers.

7. Conversion Rate:

The percentage of website visitors who complete a desired action, such as making a purchase or filling out a form. A key metric in evaluating the effectiveness of marketing campaigns.

8. Analytics:

The measurement, collection, analysis, and reporting of web data to understand and optimize digital marketing strategies. Tools like Google Analytics provide valuable insights into user behavior.

9. CTA (Call-to-Action):

A prompt that encourages the audience to take a specific action, such as clicking a button, filling out a form, or making a purchase. CTAs guide users through the desired conversion process.

10. ROI (Return on Investment):

A metric used to evaluate the profitability of an investment. In digital marketing, ROI measures the effectiveness of campaigns by comparing the cost of the campaign to the generated revenue.

11. Influencer Marketing:

Collaborating with individuals who have a significant online following (influencers) to promote a product or service. Influencer marketing leverages the influencer's credibility and reach to connect with their audience.

12. A/B Testing:

Experiment with two different versions (A and B) of a webpage or campaign to determine which performs better. A/B testing helps optimize elements like headlines, images, or CTAs for improved results.

These key concepts and terms provide a foundation for navigating the diverse landscape of digital marketing. Whether you're a beginner or a seasoned marketer, familiarity with these concepts is crucial for developing effective and informed strategies.

Chapter 2

Building a Strong Online Presence

- Website Essentials

Building a strong online presence is pivotal for businesses aiming to thrive in the digital age. A robust foundation begins with essential elements on your website:

1. User-Friendly Design:

Craft a clean, intuitive design that ensures visitors can easily navigate your site. Optimize for both desktop and mobile devices to provide a seamless user experience.

2. Compelling Homepage:

Capture attention with a visually appealing and informative homepage. Convey your brand identity, value proposition, and key offerings to engage visitors from the start.

3. Clear Navigation:

Implement a logical and user-friendly navigation structure. Visitors should effortlessly find what they're looking for, whether it's products, services, or information about your company.

4. Quality Content:

Create high-quality, relevant, and engaging content. This includes compelling copy, captivating visuals, and multimedia elements that effectively communicate your brand message.

5. SEO Optimization:

Ensure your website is optimized for search engines. Incorporate relevant keywords, meta tags, and descriptions to improve your site's visibility on search engine results pages (SERPs).

6. Fast Loading Speed:

Optimize your website's performance to minimize loading times. Visitors are more likely to stay and engage with your content if pages load quickly.

7. Mobile Responsiveness:

With an increasing number of users accessing websites on mobile devices, your site must be responsive. Ensure a seamless experience across various screen sizes.

8. Contact Information:

Display contact information, including your business address, phone number, and email. This builds trust and makes it easy for potential customers to reach you.

9. Social Media Integration:

Integrate social media buttons and feeds to encourage visitors to connect with your brand across various platforms. This fosters a broader online community and enhances your social presence.

10. Security Measures:

Prioritize the security of your website and user data. Implement SSL certificates for a secure connection, and regularly update your software to guard against potential vulnerabilities.

11. Call-to-Action (CTA):

Strategically place CTAs throughout your site to guide visitors toward desired actions, whether it's making a purchase, subscribing to a newsletter, or contacting your team.

12. Testimonials and Reviews:

Showcase positive testimonials and reviews from satisfied customers. This social proof builds credibility and trust, influencing potential customers in their decision-making process.

13. Analytics Integration:

Incorporate analytics tools like Google Analytics to track and analyze user behavior on your site. These insights are invaluable for refining your online strategy and understanding your audience.

By focusing on these website essentials, you lay the groundwork for a strong online presence. Regularly update and adapt your site to align with industry trends and evolving customer expectations, ensuring your digital footprint remains compelling and competitive.

- Content Strategy and Creation

Crafting an effective content strategy is a cornerstone of successful digital marketing. It involves thoughtful planning and execution to create content that resonates with your audience and achieves your business goals.

1. Define Your Objectives:

Clearly outline your content marketing goals. Whether it's increasing brand awareness, driving website traffic, or boosting conversions, having a clear purpose will guide your strategy.

2. Know Your Audience:

Understand your target audience's preferences, needs, and behaviors. This knowledge helps tailor your content to resonate with your audience and build a deeper connection.

3. Keyword Research:

Conduct thorough keyword research to identify relevant terms and phrases in your industry. Incorporate these keywords naturally into your content to improve search engine visibility.

4. Content Calendar:

Develop a content calendar to organize and schedule your content creation. This ensures consistency and helps you align your content with seasonal trends, events, or product launches.

5. Diverse Content Formats:

Experiment with various content formats such as blog posts, infographics, videos, podcasts, and more. Diversifying your content keeps your strategy dynamic and caters to different audience preferences.

6. Quality Over Quantity:

Prioritize quality content that provides real value to your audience. Well-researched, informative, and engaging content is more likely to capture and retain audience attention.

7. Brand Voice and Tone:

Define and maintain a consistent brand voice and tone across your content. This creates a cohesive brand identity and fosters familiarity with your audience.

8. Storytelling:

Embrace the power of storytelling. Weave narratives that captivate your audience and evoke emotions, creating a memorable and shareable experience.

9. Optimize for SEO:

Infuse your content with SEO best practices. This includes using relevant keywords, creating descriptive meta tags, and optimizing images to enhance your content's discoverability.

10. Promotion Strategy:

Develop a plan for promoting your content. Utilize social media, email marketing, influencer collaborations, and other channels to maximize the reach of your content.

11. Engagement and Interaction:

Encourage audience engagement through comments, shares, and likes. Actively respond to audience interactions to foster a sense of community around your brand.

12. Analytics and Iteration:

Regularly analyze the performance of your content using analytics tools. Assess metrics like page views, engagement rates, and conversion rates. Use these insights to refine and optimize your future content strategy.

13. Evergreen and Timely Content:

Strike a balance between evergreen content that remains relevant over time and timely content that capitalizes on current trends and events. This ensures a mix of lasting value and topical relevance.

14. User-Generated Content (UGC):

Encourage your audience to contribute to your content strategy. User-generated content, such as reviews, testimonials, or social media posts, adds authenticity and builds a sense of community.

By implementing a well-crafted content strategy, you not only enhance your online presence but also establish your brand as an authority in your industry. Adapt your strategy based on feedback, trends, and evolving consumer preferences to ensure sustained success.

- Social Media Engagement

Social media engagement is a vital aspect of any digital marketing strategy, playing a key role in building brand awareness, fostering relationships, and driving meaningful interactions with your audience. Here's how to effectively engage on social media:

1. Know Your Audience:

Understanding your audience is the foundation of successful social media engagement. Identify their preferences, interests, and behaviors to tailor your content accordingly.

2. Consistent Brand Presence:

Maintain a consistent brand presence across all social media platforms. This includes using the same profile picture, bio, and messaging to establish a cohesive and recognizable identity.

3. Interactive Content:

Create content that encourages interaction. Polls, quizzes, contests, and interactive posts prompt your audience to actively participate, increasing engagement levels.

4. Respond Promptly:

Timely responses to comments, messages, and mentions show that you value your audience. Engage in conversations, answer questions, and acknowledge feedback promptly.

5. Visual Appeal:

Leverage visually appealing content, including high-quality images and videos. Visuals capture attention and are more likely to be shared, expanding your reach.

6. Use Hashtags Strategically:

Employ relevant hashtags to increase the discoverability of your content. Research popular and niche hashtags to expand your reach and connect with a broader audience.

7. Timing Matters:

Post your content when your audience is most active. Utilize analytics tools to identify peak engagement times and schedule posts accordingly.

8. Share User-Generated Content (UGC):

Showcase content created by your audience. Reposting user-generated content not only acknowledges your community but also strengthens your brand advocacy.

9. Personalization:

Personalize your interactions. Address your audience by name when possible, and tailor content to specific segments of your audience to create a more personalized experience.

10. Embrace Trends:

Stay current with social media trends and incorporate them into your strategy. This shows your brand's relevance and willingness to engage in contemporary conversations.

11. Live Video:

Embrace live video features on platforms like Instagram, Facebook, or YouTube. Live videos provide a real-time, authentic connection with your audience, fostering engagement.

12. Community Building:

Build a sense of community among your followers. Encourage discussions, create groups or forums, and celebrate milestones to strengthen the bond between your brand and your audience.

13. Measure and Analyze:

Use analytics tools to measure the performance of your social media engagement. Track metrics such as likes, shares, comments, and click-through rates to understand what resonates best with your audience.

14. Social Listening:

Monitor social media channels for mentions of your brand, industry, or relevant keywords. Engaging in social listening allows you to respond to conversations and stay attuned to your audience's sentiments.

By implementing these strategies, you can foster a vibrant and engaged social media community. Social media engagement goes beyond numbers; it's about creating meaningful connections and nurturing a loyal audience that actively participates in and advocates for your brand.

Chapter 3.

Search Engine Optimization (SEO) Demystified

- Fundamentals of SEO

Search Engine Optimization (SEO) is a crucial aspect of digital marketing aimed at enhancing a website's visibility on search engines like Google. Understanding the fundamentals of SEO is key for anyone looking to improve their online presence. Here are some essential aspects:

1. Keywords:
   - Identify relevant keywords related to your content and business. Use tools to find

high-volume, low-competition keywords to optimize your pages effectively.

2. On-Page SEO:
   - Optimize title tags, meta descriptions, and headers with relevant keywords.
   - Ensure a clear and logical site structure for both users and search engines.
   - Create high-quality, unique content that adds value to users.

3. Off-Page SEO:
   - Build high-quality backlinks from reputable websites to improve your site's authority.
   - Engage in social media to increase brand awareness and drive traffic.

4. Technical SEO:
   - Ensure your website is mobile-friendly for a better user experience.

- Improve page speed by optimizing images, using browser caching, and minimizing code.

5. User Experience (UX):
   - Prioritize a seamless and user-friendly experience to reduce bounce rates.
   - Optimize for mobile devices, as search engines consider mobile-friendliness in rankings.

6. Content Quality:
   - Regularly update and add fresh, relevant content to your site.
   - Focus on providing comprehensive, well-researched information to become an authority in your niche.

7. Analytics and Monitoring:
   - Use tools like Google Analytics to track website performance and user behavior.
   - Monitor keyword rankings and adjust strategies based on performance data.

8. Local SEO:

- Optimize your website for local searches, including accurate business information, local keywords, and local backlinks.

9. Algorithm Updates:

- Stay informed about search engine algorithm updates to adapt your strategies accordingly.

10. Accessibility and Indexing:

- Ensure search engines can easily crawl and index your website by submitting a sitemap.

- Make sure your content is accessible to people with disabilities.

By mastering these fundamentals, you can create a solid foundation for an effective SEO strategy that improves your website's visibility, drives organic traffic, and ultimately contributes to the success of your online presence.

- On-Page and Off-Page Optimization

On-Page Optimization:

1. Title Tags:
  - Craft compelling and relevant title tags for each page, incorporating primary keywords.
    - Keep titles concise, ideally within 50-60 characters, to ensure visibility in search results.

2. Meta Descriptions:
  - Write engaging meta descriptions that provide a concise summary of the page's content.
  - Use relevant keywords naturally and encourage clicks by addressing user intent.

3. Headers (H1, H2, H3, etc.):

- Structure content with headers to improve readability and signal the hierarchy of information.

- Incorporate target keywords in headers to reinforce the page's relevance.

4. URL Structure:

- Create clean and descriptive URLs that convey the page's content.

- Include relevant keywords in the URL to enhance search engine understanding.

5. Keyword Optimization:

- Strategically place primary and secondary keywords throughout the content.

- Avoid keyword stuffing; maintain a natural and readable flow in your text.

6. Quality Content:

- Develop high-quality, valuable content that addresses user needs and concerns.

- Regularly update content to stay relevant and maintain freshness.

7. Internal Linking:
   - Implement internal links to connect related pages and guide users through your site.
   - Use descriptive anchor text that provides context for the linked content.

8. Multimedia Integration:
   - Include relevant images, videos, and other multimedia elements to enhance user engagement.
   - Optimize multimedia files for faster loading times.

9. Page Speed Optimization:
   - Optimize images, use browser caching, and minimize code to improve page loading speed.
   - Fast-loading pages contribute to a positive user experience and can positively impact rankings.

10. Mobile-Friendly Design:

- Ensure your website is responsive and provides an optimal experience on various devices.

- Google prioritizes mobile-friendly websites in search results.

Off-Page Optimization:

1. Link Building:

- Build high-quality backlinks from reputable and relevant websites.

- Focus on natural link-building strategies to enhance your site's authority.

2. Social Media Presence:

- Develop a strong presence on social media platforms to increase brand visibility.

- Social signals can indirectly impact search engine rankings.

3. Guest Posting:

- Contribute guest posts to authoritative websites in your industry.

- Include relevant links back to your site within the guest content.

4. Influencer Marketing:

- Collaborate with influencers in your niche to expand your reach.

- Influencers can contribute to the creation of valuable backlinks.

5. Online Reviews and Reputation Management:

- Encourage positive online reviews to build trust and credibility.

- Manage and respond to reviews, addressing both positive and negative feedback.

6. Social Bookmarking:

- Submit your content to social bookmarking sites to increase visibility.

- This can lead to more traffic and potential backlinks.

7. Q&A Participation:

- Engage in relevant online forums and Q&A platforms.

- Provide helpful answers and include links when appropriate.

8. Local SEO Strategies:

- Optimize your business for local searches by maintaining accurate business information.

- Get listed on local directories and optimize Google My Business.

On-page and off-page optimization work hand-in-hand to improve a website's search engine visibility and overall online performance. Balancing these strategies contributes to a well-rounded and effective SEO approach.

- SEO Best Practices

1. Keyword Research:
   - Conduct thorough keyword research to identify relevant and high-performing keywords.
   - Understand user intent behind search queries and tailor content accordingly.

2. Quality Content:
   - Prioritize creating high-quality, valuable, and unique content.
   - Focus on solving user problems, answering questions, and providing in-depth information.

3. On-Page Optimization:
   - Optimize title tags, meta descriptions, headers, and URLs for search engines and user readability.
   - Ensure a clear and logical site structure to enhance navigation.

4. Mobile-Friendly Design:

- Design a responsive website that provides a seamless experience across devices.

- Google prioritizes mobile-friendly websites in search results.

5. Page Speed:

- Optimize page loading speed by compressing images, leveraging browser caching, and minimizing code.

- Fast-loading pages enhance user experience and positively impact rankings.

6. Secure Website (HTTPS):

- Secure your website with HTTPS to ensure data integrity and build trust with users.

- Google considers HTTPS as a ranking factor.

7. Link Building:

- Focus on quality over quantity when building backlinks.

- Acquire backlinks from authoritative and relevant websites in your industry.

8. Social Signals:
- Maintain an active presence on social media platforms.
- Social signals indirectly influence search engine rankings.

9. User Experience (UX):
- Prioritize a user-friendly interface and navigation.
- Reduce bounce rates by providing a positive overall user experience.

10. Analytics and Monitoring:
- Utilize tools like Google Analytics to track website performance and user behavior.
- Regularly monitor and analyze key metrics to adjust strategies as needed.

11. Local SEO:

- Optimize for local searches by ensuring accurate business information.

 - Utilize Google My Business and get listed on relevant local directories.

12. Content Updates:

- Regularly update and refresh content to reflect industry changes and user needs.

- Google values fresh and relevant content.

13. Voice Search Optimization:

 - Consider optimizing content for voice search queries.

 - Use natural language and answer common questions concisely.

14. Schema Markup:

 - Implement schema markup to provide search engines with additional context about your content.

- Enhance the display of rich snippets in search results.

15. Avoid Black Hat SEO Tactics:

- Steer clear of unethical practices like keyword stuffing, cloaking, or buying low-quality backlinks.

- Focus on sustainable and long-term growth through ethical SEO practices.

Adhering to these SEO best practices helps establish a solid foundation for improving search engine rankings, driving organic traffic, and creating a positive online presence. Regularly adapt your strategy based on industry trends and algorithm updates to stay ahead in the dynamic landscape of SEO.

Chapter 4.

Navigating the World of Paid Advertising

- Introduction to Paid Media

In the vast landscape of digital marketing, paid advertising has emerged as a powerful tool for businesses to reach their target audiences effectively. Whether it's search engine advertising, social media promotions, or display ads, paid media offers diverse channels to amplify brand visibility. Here's an overview to help navigate the world of paid advertising:

1. Understanding Paid Media:

- Definition: Paid media involves the use of paid channels or platforms to promote and distribute content to a target audience.

- Channels: Commonly paid media channels include search engines (Google Ads), social media (Facebook Ads, Instagram Ads), display advertising, and sponsored content.

2. Key Components of Paid Advertising:

- Ad Copy: Craft compelling and concise ad copies that resonate with the target audience and encourage action.

- Visual Elements: Incorporate eye-catching visuals that align with your brand and capture attention.

- Targeting: Define specific demographics, interests, and behaviors to ensure your ads reach the right audience.

3. Paid Search Advertising:

- Platform: Google Ads is a leading paid search platform where businesses bid on keywords to have their ads appear in search results.

- Keywords: Identify relevant keywords for your business and create targeted ad campaigns around them.

- Ad Extensions: Utilize ad extensions to provide additional information and increase ad visibility.

4. Social Media Advertising:

- Platforms: Leverage social media platforms like Facebook, Instagram, Twitter, and LinkedIn for targeted advertising.

- Audience Targeting: Social media ads allow precise targeting based on demographics, interests, and user behavior.

- Ad Formats: Experiment with various ad formats such as image ads, video ads, carousel ads, and sponsored posts.

5. Display Advertising:

- Visual Appeal: Create visually appealing banner ads for placement on websites within the Google Display Network or other advertising networks.

- Remarketing: Use display ads for remarketing campaigns, targeting users who have previously interacted with your website.

6. Budgeting and Bidding:

- Setting Budgets: Establish daily or campaign budgets to control your spending.

- Bidding Strategies: Choose bidding strategies aligned with your advertising goals, such as cost-per-click (CPC), cost-per-impression (CPM), or cost-per-acquisition (CPA).

7. Measuring Performance:

- Key Metrics: Track key performance indicators (KPIs) like click-through rate (CTR), conversion rate, and return on ad spend (ROAS).

- Analytics Tools: Utilize analytics tools provided by advertising platforms to gain insights into ad performance.

8. A/B Testing:
    - Continuous Improvement: Conduct A/B testing on ad elements like headlines, images, and calls-to-action to optimize performance.
    - Data-Driven Decisions: Use test results to make data-driven decisions and refine your ad strategy.

9. Ad Compliance and Policies:
    - Ad Policies: Familiarize yourself with the ad policies of each platform to ensure compliance.
    - Quality Score: Maintain ad relevance and quality to improve your Quality Score, impacting ad placement and costs.

Navigating the world of paid advertising requires a strategic approach, continuous monitoring, and a willingness to adapt based on data and market trends. As businesses seek to connect with their audiences in a competitive digital landscape, paid media emerges as an indispensable component of a comprehensive marketing strategy.

- Google Ads and Social Media Advertising

Google Ads: Driving Targeted Traffic through Search

Introduction:
Google Ads, formerly known as Google AdWords, stands as a powerhouse in the realm of online advertising, providing businesses with a platform to

connect with potential customers through targeted and measurable campaigns.

1. Key Features of Google Ads:

- Keyword Targeting: Advertisers bid on specific keywords to display their ads in relevant search results.

- Ad Formats: Google Ads offers various ad formats, including text ads, display ads, shopping ads, and video ads.

- Location Targeting: Precise geographical targeting ensures ads reach the intended audience.

2. Search Campaigns:

- Text Ads: Craft compelling text ads with attention-grabbing headlines and concise copy.

- Ad Extensions: Utilize extensions like site links, callouts, and structured snippets to enhance ad visibility.

3. Display Network:

- Visual Ads: Reach a broader audience through visually appealing display ads on websites within the Google Display Network.

- Remarketing: Target users who have previously visited your website, reinforcing brand awareness.

4. Shopping Campaigns:

- E-commerce Focus: Ideal for businesses selling products online, showcasing products directly in search results.

- Product Listings: Display images, prices, and product information to attract potential customers.

5. Video Campaigns:

- YouTube Advertising: Tap into the vast audience on YouTube with video ads.

- Targeting Options: Refine targeting based on demographics, interests, and viewing behaviors.

6. Measuring Success:

- Conversion Tracking: Implement conversion tracking to measure the effectiveness of campaigns.

- Google Analytics Integration: Combine Google Ads with Google Analytics for comprehensive insights.

Social Media Advertising: Engaging Audiences Across Platforms

Introduction:

Social media advertising has become a cornerstone of digital marketing, allowing businesses to reach and engage their target audience on platforms like Facebook, Instagram, Twitter, LinkedIn, and more.

1. Platform Diversity:

- Facebook Ads: Leverage the extensive user base on Facebook for targeted ads based on demographics, interests, and behaviors.

- Instagram Ads: Utilize visual storytelling through photo and video ads to engage the Instagram community.

2. Audience Targeting:
   - Demographic Targeting: Specify age, gender, location, and other demographics for precise targeting.
   - Interest-Based Targeting: Reach users based on their interests, hobbies, and online behaviors.

3. Ad Formats:
   - Image Ads: Eye-catching visuals to capture attention in users' feeds.
   - Video Ads: Engage users with compelling video content that tells a story or showcases products.

4. Twitter Ads:
   - Promoted Tweets: Increase the visibility of tweets to a wider audience.

- Trend Advertising: Capitalize on trending topics to enhance reach.

5. LinkedIn Advertising:
 - Professional Audience: Target a professional audience based on job titles, industries, and company size.
- Sponsored Content: Promote content directly in the LinkedIn feed.

6. Budget Flexibility:
 - Cost-Per-Click (CPC) or Impressions (CPM): Choose between CPC and CPM models based on advertising goals and budget constraints.
 - Daily or Lifetime Budgets: Set daily or lifetime budgets to control spending.

7. Engagement and Interaction:
 - Social Engagement: Encourage likes, shares, and comments to enhance brand interaction.

- Community Building: Use social ads to foster a sense of community and brand loyalty.

8. Analytics and Insights:
  - Platform Analytics: Leverage insights provided by social media platforms for performance evaluation.
  - A/B Testing: Experiment with different ad creatives and targeting parameters to optimize campaigns.

Finally, Google Ads and social media advertising serve as dynamic tools for businesses seeking to expand their online presence and connect with their target audience. Strategic planning, creative content, and continuous optimization are key elements in harnessing the full potential of these advertising avenues. As digital landscapes evolve, combining the strengths of both Google Ads and social media advertising can create a comprehensive and effective marketing strategy.

- **Budgeting and Campaign Management**

Budgeting and campaign management are crucial elements in any successful business strategy, especially in the realm of marketing and advertising.

Budgeting:
Effective budgeting involves allocating financial resources strategically to maximize outcomes. In the context of marketing campaigns, it requires a meticulous analysis of goals, target audience, and desired outcomes. A well-structured budget ensures that resources are distributed appropriately across various channels, such as digital advertising, social media, and traditional media, to achieve optimal results.

Key aspects of budgeting include setting clear objectives, estimating costs accurately, and maintaining flexibility for unforeseen expenses. Regular monitoring and adjustments are essential to ensure that the budget aligns with the evolving needs of the campaign.

Campaign Management:

Campaign management encompasses the planning, execution, and analysis of marketing initiatives. This involves coordinating various elements such as creative development, media planning, and audience targeting. A successful campaign manager must possess a holistic view of the project, ensuring seamless collaboration between different teams.

Effective campaign management involves:

1. Strategic Planning: Develop a comprehensive strategy that aligns with the overall business goals. Identify target audiences and choose appropriate channels to reach them.

2. Execution: Implement the campaign plan efficiently, coordinating tasks and timelines. This includes creating compelling content, designing engaging visuals, and managing media placements.

3. Monitoring and Optimization: Constantly monitor the campaign's performance using relevant metrics. This data-driven approach allows for real-time adjustments, optimizing the campaign for better results.

4. Analysis and Reporting: Evaluate the campaign's success against predefined key performance indicators (KPIs). This analysis provides insights into what worked well and areas that need improvement for future campaigns.

By integrating budgeting and campaign management effectively, businesses can optimize their marketing efforts, ensuring a higher return on investment and sustained success in a competitive market.

Chapter 5.

Email Marketing Strategies

- Crafting Effective Email Campaigns

Crafting effective email campaigns is a vital component of successful email marketing strategies. It involves a thoughtful approach to content, design, and timing to engage your audience and achieve your marketing goals.

1. Define Clear Objectives:
Start by outlining the specific goals of your email campaign. Whether it's driving sales, increasing brand awareness, or fostering customer loyalty, clearly defined objectives will guide your content and design decisions.

2. Know Your Audience:

Understanding your target audience is key to creating content that resonates. Segment your email list based on demographics, preferences, or past behavior to deliver more personalized and relevant messages.

3. Compelling Subject Lines:

Craft attention-grabbing subject lines that entice recipients to open your emails. Keep them concise, compelling, and aligned with the email's content.

4. Engaging Content:

Provide valuable and engaging content that aligns with your audience's interests. Whether it's informative articles, special offers, or exclusive content, make sure it adds value and encourages further action.

5. Mobile-Friendly Design:

Given the prevalence of mobile device usage, ensure your emails are mobile-friendly. Optimize the layout and design for smaller screens to enhance the user experience.

6. Clear Call-to-Action (CTA):
Include a clear and compelling call to action that guides recipients on what to do next. Whether it's making a purchase, signing up for an event, or sharing an email, a well-crafted CTA is essential.

7. Personalization:
Personalize your emails by addressing recipients by their names and tailoring content based on their preferences or past interactions. Personalization creates a more intimate connection and increases engagement.

8. A/B Testing:
Experiment with A/B testing to understand what resonates best with your audience. Test different

elements such as subject lines, images, and CTAs to optimize your campaign for better results.

9. Optimize Sending Time:

Consider the timing of your emails to maximize open rates. Test different sending times and analyze when your audience is most responsive to fine-tune the timing of your campaigns.

10. Monitor and Analyze:

Use analytics to track the performance of your email campaigns. Monitor metrics such as open rates, click-through rates, and conversion rates. Analyzing this data provides insights into what works and allows for continuous improvement.

By implementing these strategies, businesses can create impactful email campaigns that not only capture attention but also drive meaningful engagement and conversions. Regularly refining and adapting your approach based on performance analytics ensures ongoing success in the dynamic landscape of email marketing.

- Building and Growing Your Email List

Building and growing an email list is a fundamental aspect of successful digital marketing, enabling businesses to establish direct communication with their audience. Here are essential strategies for building and expanding your email list:

1. Create Compelling Sign-Up Forms:
Design visually appealing and user-friendly sign-up forms that capture attention. Place them prominently on your website, blog, and social media channels. Communicate the value subscribers will receive.

2. Offer Incentives:

Encourage sign-ups by providing incentives such as discounts, exclusive content, or access to special promotions. People are more likely to share their email addresses when they perceive added value.

3. Implement Landing Pages:

Design dedicated landing pages for specific campaigns or promotions. These pages should focus on the benefits of subscribing and make the sign-up process straightforward.

4. Leverage Content Marketing:

Create high-quality, valuable content to attract and engage your target audience. Include strategically placed opt-in opportunities within blog posts, articles, and other content.

5. Utilize Social Media:

Promote your email sign-up across your social media platforms. Use compelling visuals and concise messages to encourage followers to join your mailing list.

6. Host Webinars and Events:
Organize webinars, workshops, or virtual events related to your industry. Require participants to provide their email addresses for registration, expanding your list with engaged individuals.

7. Optimize Website Pop-Ups:
Implement exit-intent pop-ups or timed pop-ups on your website. Use these strategically to capture visitors' attention before they leave and entice them to subscribe.

8. Run Contests and Giveaways:
Hold contests or giveaways with entry requirements that include subscribing to your email list. This not only attracts new subscribers but also generates excitement around your brand.

9. Collaborate with Influencers:
Partner with influencers or industry experts to extend your reach. Influencers can introduce your brand to their followers, potentially driving more subscribers to your email list.

10. Use Referral Programs:
Encourage your existing subscribers to refer others by implementing a referral program. Offer rewards or exclusive content to both the referrer and the new subscriber.

11. Employ E-commerce Strategies:
For e-commerce businesses, strategically place opt-in forms during the checkout process. Offer incentives like order updates, exclusive promotions, or loyalty programs to encourage sign-ups.

12. Ensure GDPR Compliance:
When collecting email addresses, prioritize user privacy and comply with data protection

regulations. Communicate how you will use their information and provide an option to opt out.

Building and growing your email list requires a combination of creativity, strategic planning, and ongoing optimization. By consistently delivering value and engaging with your audience, you can foster a strong and responsive email community that contributes to the overall success of your marketing efforts.

- Automation and Personalization

Automation and personalization are two integral components of modern marketing strategies, working hand in hand to enhance efficiency and create more meaningful connections with target audiences.

Automation:

1. Workflow Streamlining:

Automation involves streamlining repetitive tasks and workflows, saving time and resources. In marketing, this can include automating email campaigns, social media posts, and customer follow-ups.

2. Data Analysis and Insights:

Automated tools can analyze vast amounts of data quickly, providing valuable insights into customer behavior, preferences, and engagement patterns. This data-driven approach enables marketers to make informed decisions.

3. Lead Nurturing:

Automation is instrumental in lead nurturing. It allows businesses to deliver targeted content at specific stages of the customer journey, guiding leads through the sales funnel more effectively.

4. Behavior-Based Triggers:

Set up automated triggers based on user behavior, such as website visits or interactions with emails. This ensures timely and relevant communication, increasing the chances of conversion.

5. Social Media Scheduling:

Automate social media posts to maintain a consistent online presence. This ensures that your brand remains visible across platforms without the need for constant manual intervention.

Personalization:

1. Tailored Content:

Personalization involves customizing content to meet the individual preferences and interests of your audience. This can range from personalized product recommendations to tailored email content.

2. Dynamic Website Content:

Implement dynamic content on your website that adapts based on user behavior and preferences. This creates a more personalized and engaging experience for visitors.

3. Email Personalization:

Craft personalized email campaigns by addressing recipients by name and tailoring content based on their past interactions with your brand. Personalized emails have higher open and click-through rates.

4. Recommendation Engines:

Use recommendation engines to suggest products or content based on users' previous behavior. This enhances the user experience and can lead to increased sales and engagement.

5. Segmentation Strategies:

Segment your audience based on demographics, behavior, or other relevant factors. This allows for more targeted and personalized communication, resonating better with different audience segments.

6. Personalized Ads:

Leverage personalization in advertising by delivering targeted ads to specific audience segments. This increases the relevance of your ads and improves the chances of conversion.

7. Interactive Content:

Implement interactive content, such as quizzes or surveys, that adapts based on user responses. This not only provides a personalized experience but also gathers valuable insights.

By combining automation and personalization, businesses can create more efficient and effective marketing strategies. Automated processes streamline operations, while personalization ensures that the content and interactions are tailored to the unique preferences of each individual, fostering stronger connections and driving better results.

Chapter 6.

Measuring Success with Analytics

- Importance of Analytics in Digital Marketing

Analytics plays a pivotal role in measuring success, especially in the realm of digital marketing. By leveraging data-driven insights, businesses can gauge the effectiveness of their strategies, campaigns, and overall online presence.

1. Informed Decision-Making: Analytics empower marketers to make informed decisions by providing a comprehensive view of user behavior,

engagement, and conversion rates. This data-driven approach ensures that marketing efforts are aligned with actual user preferences and trends.

2. Performance Evaluation: Through analytics, businesses can assess the performance of their digital marketing initiatives in real time. Metrics such as website traffic, click-through rates, and conversion rates offer a quantitative understanding of campaign success, allowing for quick adjustments or optimizations.

3. Targeted Marketing: Analytics enable precise audience targeting. By analyzing demographic data, user behavior, and preferences, marketers can tailor their campaigns to specific segments, ensuring that resources are allocated effectively and messages resonate with the intended audience.

4. ROI Measurement: Measuring return on investment (ROI) is crucial for any marketing

strategy. Analytics provide insights into the financial impact of campaigns, helping businesses identify which channels or tactics deliver the best results and optimizing budgets accordingly.

5. Continuous Improvement: Successful digital marketing is an iterative process. Analytics facilitate continuous improvement by revealing areas for enhancement. Whether it's refining ad copy, adjusting targeting parameters, or optimizing landing pages, data-driven insights drive ongoing refinement and growth.

6. User Experience Optimization: Analytics help businesses understand how users interact with their digital assets. By analyzing user journeys, businesses can identify pain points, optimize website navigation, and enhance overall user experience, leading to higher satisfaction and increased conversions.

7. Adaptability: In the dynamic digital landscape, adaptability is key. Analytics provide the necessary intelligence to adapt marketing strategies based on changing trends, consumer behavior, and competitive landscapes, ensuring that businesses stay ahead of the curve.

8. Attribution Modeling: Understanding the customer journey is vital for attributing success to various touchpoints. Analytics allow marketers to employ attribution models, assigning value to each interaction, and comprehensively attributing conversions to specific channels or campaigns.

In essence, the importance of analytics in digital marketing cannot be overstated. It serves as the compass guiding marketing efforts, helping businesses navigate the digital landscape, make informed decisions, and ultimately achieve and measure success in a data-driven manner.

- Setting and Monitoring Key Performance Indicators (KPIs)

Setting and monitoring Key Performance Indicators (KPIs) is essential for organizations to measure their progress toward specific goals and objectives. KPIs are quantifiable metrics that reflect the critical success factors of a business or project. Here's a breakdown of the process:

Setting KPIs:

1. Define Objectives:

Clearly outline the overarching goals and objectives that align with the organization's mission and strategy.

2. Identify Critical Success Factors:

Determine the factors crucial to achieving the defined objectives. These can be related to sales, customer satisfaction, efficiency, or any other relevant aspect.

3. Select Relevant Metrics:

Choose specific, measurable metrics that directly reflect progress toward each critical success factor. Avoid selecting too many KPIs to maintain focus.

4. Ensure SMART Criteria:

KPIs should be Specific, Measurable, Achievable, Relevant, and Time-bound. This ensures clarity and helps in effective measurement.

5. Align with Stakeholders:

Collaborate with key stakeholders to ensure that the selected KPIs resonate with their expectations and contribute to overall success.

Monitoring KPIs:

1. Establish Baselines:

Before implementing changes, establish baseline measurements for each KPI to understand the current state. This provides a reference point for evaluating progress.

2. Implement Tracking Systems:

Utilize technology and systems to track KPIs in real time. This may involve implementing software solutions or creating manual tracking processes, depending on the nature of the metrics.

3. Regular Review and Analysis:

Conduct regular reviews of KPI data. Analyze trends, patterns, and any deviations from the expected outcomes. This ongoing analysis allows for timely adjustments and improvements.

4. Feedback Loops:

Establish feedback loops to gather insights from teams and departments. This information can highlight challenges or opportunities that may impact KPI performance.

5. Adaptation and Improvement:

KPIs are not static; they may need adjustment based on changing business environments or strategies. Be open to refining or adding new KPIs to ensure they remain relevant.

6. Communication and Transparency:

Communicate KPI results transparently within the organization. This fosters accountability and encourages collective efforts toward achieving the established goals.

7. Celebrate Successes and Address Challenges:

Acknowledge and celebrate achievements when KPIs are met. Simultaneously, address challenges promptly, seeking solutions to prevent persistent issues.

By effectively setting and monitoring KPIs, organizations can enhance decision-making processes, stay agile in dynamic environments, and continually strive for improvement.

- Continuous Improvement and Adaptation

Continuous improvement and adaptation are integral aspects of personal and professional growth. Embracing a mindset of continuous improvement involves a commitment to evaluating, refining, and enhancing one's skills, processes, and knowledge over time. This approach fosters resilience and agility, enabling individuals and organizations to navigate the ever-evolving challenges of today's dynamic world.

In a professional context, continuous improvement entails regularly assessing and optimizing workflows, identifying areas for enhancement, and implementing positive changes. This iterative process not only increases efficiency but also contributes to a culture of innovation and excellence within a team or organization. It encourages employees to seek ongoing learning opportunities, stay abreast of industry trends, and proactively adapt to changing circumstances.

Adaptation, on the other hand, is the ability to adjust to new conditions and circumstances. In a rapidly changing environment, being adaptable is crucial for success. This involves not only reacting effectively to unexpected challenges but also anticipating and preparing for future changes. Individuals who embrace adaptation demonstrate resilience, resourcefulness, and a willingness to step out of their comfort zones.

The synergy between continuous improvement and adaptation creates a powerful combination of personal and professional development. Those who actively seek ways to enhance their skills and processes are better equipped to navigate uncertainties and capitalize on emerging opportunities. Flexibility and a growth mindset are key components of this dynamic approach, allowing individuals and organizations to thrive in an ever-changing landscape.

Continuous improvement and adaptation are indispensable elements in the effective deployment of analytics within digital marketing strategies. This dynamic approach ensures that businesses remain agile, responsive, and ahead of the curve in an ever-evolving online landscape.

1. Data-Driven Iteration: Analytics provides a wealth of data, and leveraging this information for iterative improvements is fundamental. By regularly

analyzing performance metrics, marketers can identify trends, anomalies, and areas for enhancement, leading to a continuous cycle of refinement.

2. A/B Testing for Optimization: A/B testing, or split testing, is a valuable technique facilitated by analytics. Marketers can experiment with variations in elements such as ad copies, visuals, or calls-to-action and rely on analytics to measure the impact on user engagement and conversion rates. This iterative testing approach allows for data-backed optimizations.

3. Real-Time Monitoring: The real-time nature of analytics tools enables marketers to monitor campaign performance as it unfolds. This immediacy empowers quick responses to emerging trends or unexpected challenges, ensuring that marketing strategies can be adapted on the fly for optimal results.

4. Machine Learning and Predictive Analytics: Integrating machine learning algorithms and predictive analytics into digital marketing analytics enhances adaptability. These technologies analyze historical data to predict future trends and behaviors, allowing marketers to proactively adjust strategies based on anticipated changes in consumer preferences or market dynamics.

5. Multi-Channel Integration: Digital marketing often involves multiple channels, from social media to email campaigns. Integrating analytics across these channels provides a holistic view of the customer journey. Marketers can then adapt strategies based on cross-channel insights, ensuring a cohesive and synchronized approach.

6. Evolving Audience Insights: Consumer behavior evolves, and analytics help marketers stay attuned to these changes. By continually updating audience

personas and adjusting targeting criteria, businesses can ensure that their messaging remains relevant and resonant with the ever-changing preferences of their target audience.

7. Feedback Loop Integration: The feedback loop between analytics and marketing strategies is critical. Actively soliciting and analyzing feedback, whether from customer interactions or campaign performance, creates a continuous loop of improvement. This iterative process ensures that marketing efforts align with customer expectations and market dynamics.

8. Scalability and Flexibility: Digital marketing campaigns vary in scale and scope. Analytics platforms that are scalable and adaptable accommodate the changing needs of campaigns. Whether it's scaling up for a major product launch or pivoting strategy due to unforeseen

circumstances, the flexibility of analytics tools is a cornerstone of effective campaign management.

In essence, the continuous improvement and adaptation of analytics in digital marketing are essential for staying competitive and relevant. Embracing a mindset of ongoing refinement, informed by data-driven insights, ensures that marketing strategies not only meet current objectives but also remain adaptable to future challenges and opportunities in the ever-evolving digital landscape.